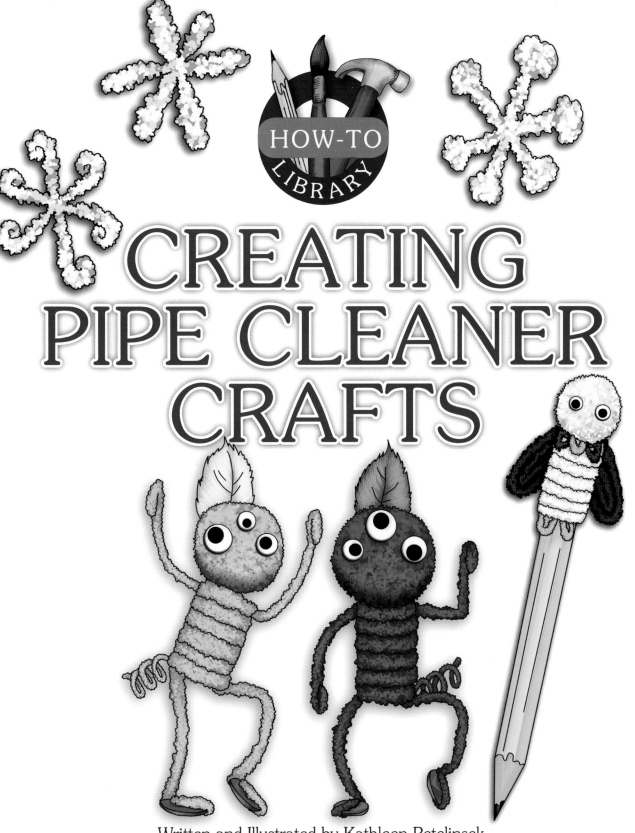

CREATING PIPE CLEANER CRAFTS

Written and Illustrated by Kathleen Petelinsek

CHERRY LAKE PUBLISHING • ANN ARBOR, MICHIGAN

A NOTE TO ADULTS:
Please review the instructions for these craft projects before your children make them. Be sure to help them with any steps you do not think they can safely do on their own.

A NOTE TO KIDS:
Be sure to ask an adult for help with these craft activities when you need it. Always put your safety first!

Published in the United States of America by Cherry Lake Publishing
Ann Arbor, Michigan
www.cherrylakepublishing.com

Photo Credits: Page 4, ©siamionau pavel/Shutterstock.com; page 5, ©Jacqui Martin/Shutterstock.com; page 6, ©mark higgins/Shutterstock.com; page 7, ©rSnapshotPhotos/Shutterstock.com; page 29, ©Dragon Images/Shutterstock.com.

Library of Congress Cataloging-in-Publication Data
Petelinsek, Kathleen.
  Creating pipe cleaner crafts / by Kathleen Petelinsek.
      pages cm — (Crafts) (How-to library)
  Includes bibliographical references and index.
  ISBN 978-1-63137-784-6 (lib. bdg.) — ISBN 978-1-63137-844-7 (ebook)
— ISBN 978-1-63137-804-1 (pbk.) — ISBN 978-1-63137-824-9 (pdf)
  1. Pipe cleaner craft—Juvenile literature. I. Title.
  TT880.P48 2014
  745.5—dc23   2014002058

Cherry Lake Publishing would like to acknowledge the work of
The Partnership for 21st Century Skills. Please visit www.p21.org
for more information.

Printed in the United States of America
Corporate Graphics Inc.
July 2014

HOW-TO LIBRARY

TABLE OF CONTENTS

Pipes and Pipe Cleaners

Pipe cleaners were originally created as useful tools for cleaning tight, curved spaces.

Have you ever seen a pipe cleaner? These fuzzy, bendable devices have a unique quality that makes them good for cleaning small, curved spaces where no other tools will fit. They were originally invented to clean the inside of tobacco pipes. Before the invention of the pipe cleaner, smokers used feathers to clean their pipes. If you think about it, a bird feather is very similar to a pipe cleaner. They both have a flexible but sturdy base that is covered with a soft, absorbent material.

John Harry Stedman and Charles Angel of Rochester, New York, invented the pipe cleaner in the early 1900s. Their device was made of **chenille** wrapped around a very thin wire.

Pipe smoking is no longer as popular as it once was. People have learned that smoking is very bad for you. However, pipe cleaners are still easy to find in stores. This is because people use them in a wide variety of crafting projects!

Pipe cleaners can be bent and twisted into a variety of fun shapes.

Beyond Cleaning Pipes

Pipe cleaners come in a huge variety of colors.

Crafting pipe cleaners are typically longer and thicker than the ones invented by Stedman and Angel. They come in a wide variety of colors. Crafting pipe cleaners are not usually made from chenille. They are made with **polyester** or **nylon** instead. Some crafting pipe cleaners even have **tinsel** wrapped around them to make them sparkle. Nylon, polyester, and tinsel are not good at absorbing moisture. This means they aren't very good for cleaning pipes. However, they are great for making crafts!

You can make just about anything you can imagine with these colorful, bendable tools. Pipe cleaners can be bent into toys, jewelry, and napkin holders. You can decorate gifts with them or add flair to your hair.

As you come up with ideas for new pipe cleaner projects, draw them in a sketchbook. Then you can look at your drawings for **inspiration** when you are ready to create a new project!

You can use pipe cleaners to create one-of-a-kind crafts.

Pipe Cleaners and Other Materials

Pipe cleaners are found at most craft stores. You can also find them at many department stores. They come in a variety of colors, textures, thicknesses, and lengths. They are often sold in variety packs, which is a great way to get started.

To start crafting with pipe cleaners, you will want a variety of colors and lengths to choose from. It is also helpful to have a few other supplies on hand. Below is a list of some of the materials you will need to complete the projects in this book.

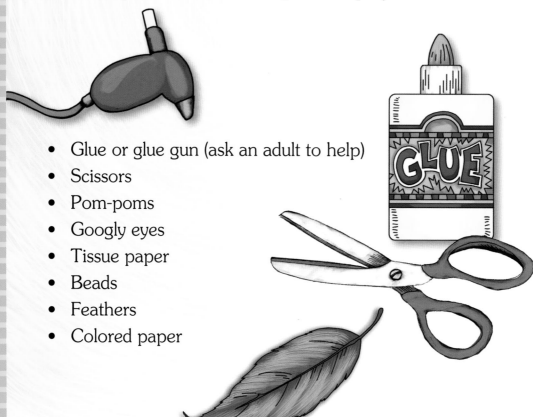

- Glue or glue gun (ask an adult to help)
- Scissors
- Pom-poms
- Googly eyes
- Tissue paper
- Beads
- Feathers
- Colored paper

- Egg carton
- Paint and paintbrushes
- Old newspapers

Check the instructions before starting each craft to see if you need additional supplies. Keeping a variety of materials on hand gives you endless possibilities for creating.

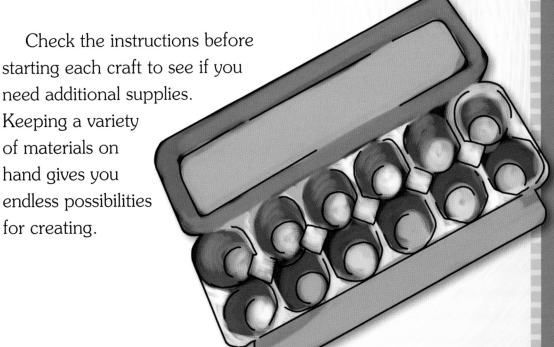

Bouquet of Poppies

These flowers will never wilt! Use them to decorate your room or as a centerpiece at the dinner table.

Materials

- Egg carton
- Old newspaper
- Green paint
- Paintbrushes and water
- Scissors
- Colored tissue paper
- Pipe cleaners
- Vase

Steps

1. Cut your egg carton into 12 separate egg cups.
2. Spread the old newspaper out on your work surface to protect it. Paint your egg cups green. Let them dry.
3. Cut your tissue paper into circles with a 6-inch (15 cm) **diameter**. You will need two tissue paper circles for each egg cup.

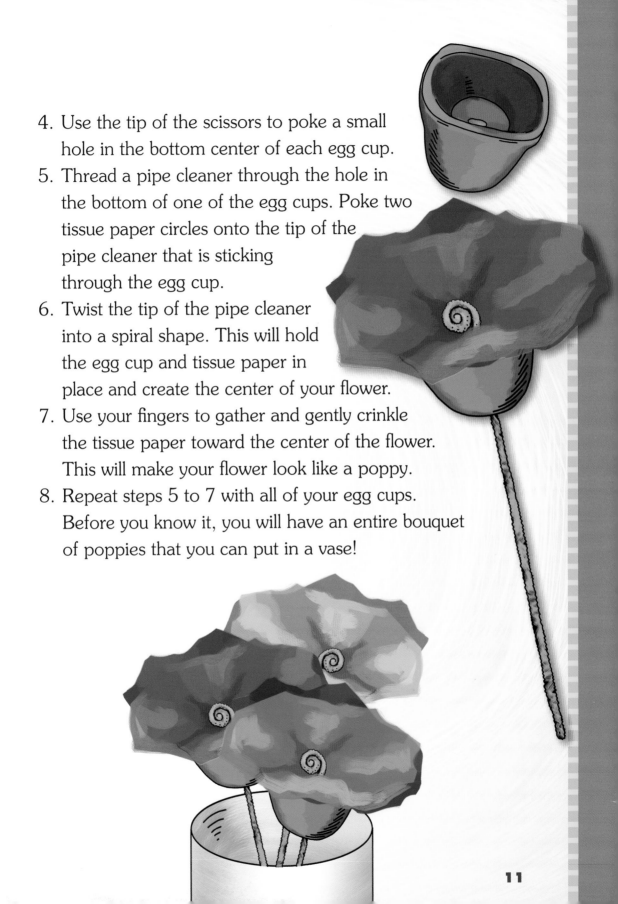

4. Use the tip of the scissors to poke a small hole in the bottom center of each egg cup.

5. Thread a pipe cleaner through the hole in the bottom of one of the egg cups. Poke two tissue paper circles onto the tip of the pipe cleaner that is sticking through the egg cup.

6. Twist the tip of the pipe cleaner into a spiral shape. This will hold the egg cup and tissue paper in place and create the center of your flower.

7. Use your fingers to gather and gently crinkle the tissue paper toward the center of the flower. This will make your flower look like a poppy.

8. Repeat steps 5 to 7 with all of your egg cups. Before you know it, you will have an entire bouquet of poppies that you can put in a vase!

11

Dancing Monsters

These zany monsters are a lot of fun to play with. Make them look as wild as possible by using thick, colorful pipe cleaners.

Materials
- Scissors
- 3 (12-inch, or 30 cm) pipe cleaners
- Pencil
- Wide marker
- 2 pennies
- Glue gun
- 3 googly eyes
- 1 medium pom-pom
- Feather

Steps
1. Use the scissors to cut one pipe cleaner into two pieces. One piece should be 7 inches (18 cm) long. The other should be 5 inches (13 cm) long.
2. Cut a second pipe cleaner to a length of 9 inches (23 cm).
3. Twist the center point of the 7-inch (18 cm) pipe cleaner around one end of the remaining 12-inch (30 cm) pipe cleaner. A couple of twists is all you need. These will be your monster's arms.

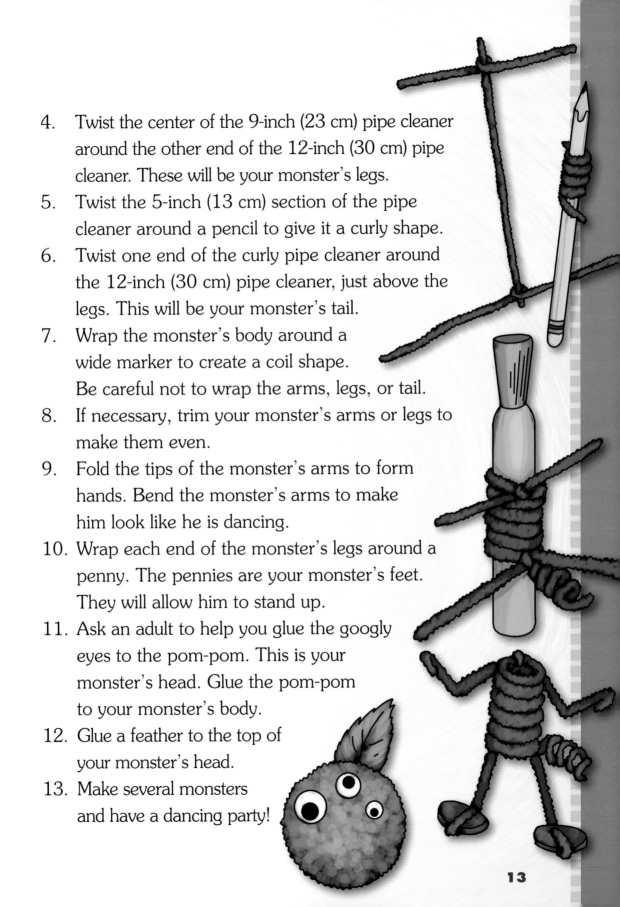

4. Twist the center of the 9-inch (23 cm) pipe cleaner around the other end of the 12-inch (30 cm) pipe cleaner. These will be your monster's legs.

5. Twist the 5-inch (13 cm) section of the pipe cleaner around a pencil to give it a curly shape.

6. Twist one end of the curly pipe cleaner around the 12-inch (30 cm) pipe cleaner, just above the legs. This will be your monster's tail.

7. Wrap the monster's body around a wide marker to create a coil shape. Be careful not to wrap the arms, legs, or tail.

8. If necessary, trim your monster's arms or legs to make them even.

9. Fold the tips of the monster's arms to form hands. Bend the monster's arms to make him look like he is dancing.

10. Wrap each end of the monster's legs around a penny. The pennies are your monster's feet. They will allow him to stand up.

11. Ask an adult to help you glue the googly eyes to the pom-pom. This is your monster's head. Glue the pom-pom to your monster's body.

12. Glue a feather to the top of your monster's head.

13. Make several monsters and have a dancing party!

Princes and Princesses

Be royalty for a day with this jeweled crown!

Materials

- 6 to 12 pipe cleaners in a variety of colors (ones with tinsel in them work great)
- Beads

Steps

1. Twist two pipe cleaners together at the ends. Twist the other ends together to form a circle. It should fit around your head. Adjust the size of the circle to make sure it fits properly. Use a third pipe cleaner if you need to.

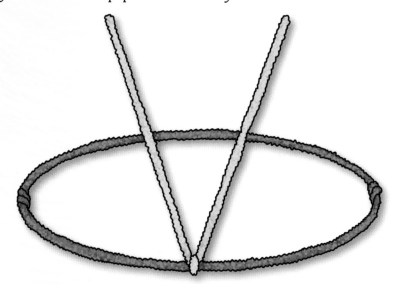

2. Bend a pipe cleaner in half and secure the center point to your circle with a couple of twists.
3. Add beads to each side of the bent pipe cleaner.
4. Bend the middle of each side of the twisted pipe cleaner and twist it back onto the circle. You should have two points now.
5. Repeat steps 2 to 4 until you have points all the way around the circle.
6. Place the crown on your head and become a prince or princess!

TIP
Be creative with how you make your points and where you place your beads. This will allow you to create many different crown shapes.

Personalized Cards

Create your own customized stamps and use them to print colorful greeting cards for your friends and family!

Materials

- Heavy paper and matching envelopes
- Ruler
- Scissors
- Pencil
- Cardboard
- Old newspapers
- 6 to 12 pipe cleaners
- Glue gun
- Paint
- Sturdy paper or Styrofoam plate

Steps

1. Start by creating a card that will fit inside your envelope. Measure your envelope. Now measure and cut your paper into a rectangle that is the same width and twice the height of the envelope.
2. Fold the cut paper in half. Check to make sure your card fits into your envelope. Trim the edges if you need to. Set your card and envelope aside.

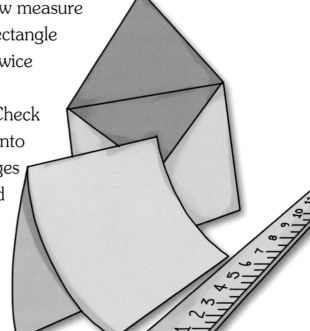

3. Mark and cut your cardboard to match the size of your envelope.

4. Spread old newspapers over your work surface.

5. Bend your pipe cleaners into flat shapes. You can make curlicues or any other design you can think of. You can even shape your pipe cleaners into letters and words.

6. Ask an adult to help you glue your pipe cleaner designs to the cardboard. If you are including letters or words, glue them on so they read backward.

7. Pour a small amount of paint onto your plate. Dip the pipe cleaner side of your cardboard into the paint. Make sure the entire design is covered in paint.

8. Stamp your design onto an old piece of paper to see how it looks. If you like it, stamp the front of your card.

9. To be really creative, you can press multiple stamps onto a single card. Use a different color of paint for each stamp. Be sure to let the paint dry in between stamps.

Decorate with a Vine

Create a twisty vine you can use to decorate your room.
No need to water it—this plant will last all year!

Materials

- 10 or more colored pipe cleaners (flower colors)
- Thick marker
- 20 or more green pipe cleaners
- Pencil

NOTE
The more pipe cleaners you have, the longer your vine can be.

Steps

1. Twist the ends of two flower-colored pipe cleaners together with a couple of twists.
2. Wrap the two pipe cleaners around a thick marker to create a spiral. Remove the spiral from the marker.
3. Bring the two loose ends of your spiral together and twist. This will form a curly flower.

4. Put one green pipe cleaner through one of the loops of the flower. Twist the green pipe cleaner to the flower at the center point of the green pipe cleaner to secure it.

5. Bend each side of the green pipe cleaner back to its center and twist it where you secured it to the flower to hold it in place. Shape the two folded ends into leaves.

6. Repeat steps 1 to 5 to make more flowers.

7. Thread a green pipe cleaner through the center of a flower and leaf, twisting it to a loop in the flower to secure it. This green pipe cleaner is the vine. Repeat for each flower.

8. Twist the green vine ends together to make a long vine.

9. Twist more green pipe cleaners around a pencil to create short, curly vines. Attach the curly vines to the long vine.

10. Wrap your vine around a window or along your bed frame for a colorful decoration.

Snowflake Light Catchers

These snowflakes won't melt when the sun comes out! Hang them around your house as fun winter decorations.

Materials

- Pipe cleaners
- Scissors
- 12-inch (30 cm) string
- Pencil
- Wide mouthed jar or bowl
- 1 cup boiling water
- 3 tablespoons Borax powder
- Blue food coloring (optional)

Steps

1. Cut a pipe cleaner into three equal parts. Twist each of them together at the centers to form a six-point star. Trim the points to make them equal in length. If you want a more complicated snowflake shape, you can twist more pipe cleaners onto your design. Try twisting small pieces onto the longer points of your snowflake. Do not make your light catcher larger than the mouth of your jar or bowl, though. It needs to fit in your container.

2. When you are done, tie a string around one of the points of the light catcher. Tie a pencil to the other end of the string.

3. Ask an adult to help you fill the jar or bowl with boiling water. Add Borax to the water one tablespoon at a time. Stir to dissolve as you add each spoonful.

4. If you would like a colored light catcher, add a few drops of blue food coloring to the water and stir.

5. Add the light catcher to the liquid so that the pencil rests on top of the jar or bowl. The light catcher should be completely covered with liquid and hanging freely. It should not touch the sides or bottom of your container. Allow it to sit overnight.

6. When you wake up, you will have a crystallized snowflake. Remove it from the container and allow it to dry. Now hang it in your window to catch the light!

TIP
Can you think of other shapes that you can crystallize? You could also add different colors of food coloring to your Borax mixture.

A Proper Penguin Pencil Topper

This penguin friend will keep you company while you do your homework or draw new craft ideas in your sketchbook.

Materials

- 1 orange pipe cleaner
- Pencil
- 1 white pipe cleaner
- 1 black pipe cleaner
- Ruler
- Scissors
- Glue gun
- 1 white pom-pom
- 2 googly eyes

Steps

1. Cut the orange pipe cleaner to a length of 5 inches (13 cm). Set it alongside the pencil, with the tip of the pipe cleaner at the eraser end of the pencil.
2. Wrap a white pipe cleaner around the orange pipe cleaner and the pencil. One inch (2.5 cm) of orange pipe cleaner should stick out from the white pipe cleaner on the eraser end. Two and a half inches (6 cm) should stick out from the wrapped white pipe cleaner on the other end.

3. Bend the 1-inch (2.5 cm) section of the orange pipe cleaner to form a beak.

4. Bend the other section of orange pipe cleaner into two loops to form feet.

5. Measure and cut the black pipe cleaner to a length of 8 inches (20 cm).

6. Insert the black pipe cleaner under the orange beak and over the top of the eraser. Leave 2 inches (5 cm) of pipe cleaner under the beak.

7. Bend the 2-inch (5 cm) section of black pipe cleaner to form a black bow tie.

8. Bend the remaining 6 inches (15 cm) of black pipe cleaner to form the penguin's wings.

9. Ask an adult to help you glue a white pom-pom to the top of the spiral and orange beak.

10. Glue googly eyes to the pom-pom.

TIP

What other creatures can you create to top your pencils? Be creative and draw your ideas in your sketchbook.

Summer Is Here!

Butterflies are a sure sign that summer has arrived. These pipe cleaner butterflies hang from a branch and can remind you of summer all year long.

Materials

- 12–15 pipe cleaners
- 20–30 beads (various sizes)
- Tree branch
- Vase (optional)
- String

Steps

1. Fold one of your pipe cleaners in half.
2. Thread four beads onto one-half of the pipe cleaner. This will be your butterfly's body. Secure the beads by twisting the pipe cleaner together once or twice.
3. Twist the center of two other pipe cleaners around the folded pipe cleaner at the point where you secured the beads with a twist.

4. Loop the two pipe cleaners on both sides to create four wings. Twist the ends to secure them.

5. Thread one larger bead onto your original folded pipe cleaner right above the wings. This will be your butterfly's head. Secure the bead with one or two twists.

6. You should have two ends remaining from your original folded pipe cleaner. These are your butterfly's antennae. Curl each of the ends into a small spiral.

7. Repeat steps 1 to 6 to create more butterflies.

8. Put your tree branch into a vase to hold it upright or tie a string to it and hang it from the ceiling like a mobile.

9. Cut a 12-inch (30 cm) length of string and tie one end to one of your butterflies. Now tie the other end to the branch. Hang all of your butterflies from the branch.

Thanksgiving Napkin Holders

These napkin holders will give your family's dinner table a festive look on turkey day.

Materials

- 2 orange pipe cleaners
- 1 red pipe cleaner
- Napkin
- Glue gun
- 1 large brown pom-pom
- 2 googly eyes
- 1 yellow pipe cleaner

Steps

1. Twist one of the orange pipe cleaners and the red pipe cleaner around each other. Stop twisting when you have 3 inches (7.5 cm) of pipe cleaner remaining.

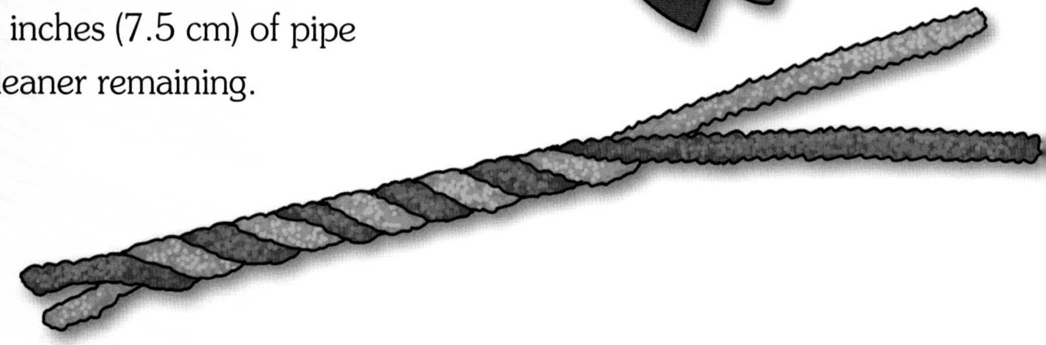

2. Grab your napkin from the center and hold it up so the four corners drape down. Gather it together.

3. Wrap the orange and red twisted section around the gathered napkin and twist it together into a loop. Secure it by twisting it a few times.

4. Bend the loose red end to form the turkey's wattle.

5. Bend the loose orange end to form the turkey's beak.

6. Secure the other orange pipe cleaner to the napkin ring at its center point with a few twists.

7. Bend each side of the orange pipe cleaner around into a loop to form tail feathers. Press the tail feathers flat against the napkin. The turkey's beak and wattle should be in front of the feathers and not pressed flat.

8. Repeat steps 6 and 7 with the yellow pipe cleaner.

9. Ask an adult to help you glue the pom-pom to the tail feathers behind the beak and wattle. Adjust the position of your turkey's beak and wattle if you need to.
10. Glue googly eyes to your turkey's face.

TIP
What other holidays can you create a napkin holder for? How about a reindeer for Christmas? Hearts for Valentine's Day? Be creative!

More Ideas

As you twisted your way through the crafts in this book, you probably discovered that the things you can make with pipe cleaners are endless. With a few pipe cleaners and some beads, you can make a necklace, a bracelet, or a ring. Create a pair of glasses with a few twists. If you have long hair, braid a pipe cleaner into one of your braids. Now you can twist your braids into crazy shapes!

Search the Web for other ideas and sketch them in your sketchbook. Sketching your ideas helps you plan how to create your pipe cleaner craft. It also allows you to think about your project and change it to make it even better. You can use your sketchbook to make lists of materials you will need for each project. Perhaps one day you can turn your sketchbook into a book like this one!

Try looking online to find new ideas for craft projects.

Glossary

chenille (shuh-NEEL) a soft material that is good at absorbing moisture

diameter (dye-AM-uh-tur) a straight line through the center of a circle, connecting opposite sides

inspiration (in-spuh-RAY-shuhn) something that gives you an idea, emotion, or attitude

nylon (NYE-lahn) a strong artificial fiber used to make things such as clothing, carpets, and rope

polyester (pah-lee-ES-tur) a man-made substance that is used to make plastic products and fabric

tinsel (TIN-suhl) strands of sparkling, decorative material that are often used to decorate Christmas trees

For More Information

Books

Boutique-sha of Japan. *Making Pipe Cleaner Pets*. East Petersburg, PA: Design Originals, 2010.

Steele-Saccio, Eva. *Twisted Critters: The Pipe Cleaner Book*. Palo Alto, CA: Klutz, 2011.

Web Sites

Martha Stewart's Crafts for Kids: Pipe Cleaner Pals How-To
www.parents.com/fun/arts-crafts/kid/martha-stewart-pipe-cleaner-pals/
Do you like animals? Visit this site for directions on how to make some pipe cleaner animal pals.

Spoonful—25 Easy DIY Pipe Cleaner Activities for Kids
http://spoonful.com/crafts/25-easy-diy-pipe-cleaner-activities-kids
This site offers a bunch of ideas for pipe cleaner crafts and games.

Index

About the Author

Kathleen Petelinsek is a children's book illustrator, writer, and designer. As a child, she spent her summers drawing and painting. She still loves to do the same today, but now all her work is done on the computer. When she isn't working on her computer, she can be found outside swimming, biking, running, or playing in the snow of southern Minnesota.